you'll get through this

you'll get through this

HOPE AND HELP FOR YOUR TURBULENT TIMES

MAX LUCADO

WRITTEN BY KEVIN AND SHERRY HARNEY

THOMAS NELSON
Since 1798

NASHVILLE   DALLAS   MEXICO CITY   RIO DE JANEIRO

Published in Nashville, Tennessee, by Thomas Nelson. Thomas Nelson is a registered trademark of Thomas Nelson, Inc.

Published in association with Anvil II Management, Ltd.

Thomas Nelson, Inc. titles may be purchased in bulk for educational, business, fund-raising, or sales promotional use. For information, please e-mail SpecialMarkets@ThomasNelson.com.

ISBN 978-0-8499-5998-1

Printed in the United States of America

13 14 15 16 17 RRD 9 8 7 6 5 4 3 2 1

Contents

Of Note

The quotations interspersed throughout this study guide are excerpts from the book *You'll Get Through This* by Max Lucado and from the video curriculum of the same name. All other resources—including the introductions, small group questions, between-sessions materials, and the small group leader helps—have been written by Kevin and Sherry Harney.

Hitting the Wall

Marathoners call it "hitting the wall." They come to a point where their bodies say, "No more." Their legs feel like they are made of lead. Their respiratory systems scream, "Stop!"

Triathletes call it "bonking." As they swim, then ride, and finally run, they feel their bodies begin to shut down. They've "bonked."

You don't have to be an extreme athlete to know how it feels to hit a point where it seems you simply can't press on.

Brenda has lovingly walked beside her husband for years, poured her life into the family, and cared as best she can. Then she discovers that the man who said, "I do," no longer does. She wonders, "How can I make it through this? Can I go on? Will I survive another day?"

Daniel has worked for the company for two decades. He has given his heart, soul, and countless late nights and weekends to help the business increase its bottom line. Now he stands at his car, a box of items from his desk in his arms. With no warning, he has been informed that his services are no longer required and walked out of the building by security. He's in shock. "What will

I tell my wife and kids? How will I pay the bills? Can we survive this?"

Curtis lives for the Friday night lights. Football is not just a sport; it is the air he breathes. He has offers for college scholarships and his stock is rising. Late in the game, as a defensive end tackles him at the end of a run, he feels a searing pain run through his leg and hears a snap, loud as a firecracker. While being wheeled to the ambulance, his mind races: "What if I can't play for the rest of the season? What if I don't get a scholarship? I can't imagine my life without football; can I make it through this?"

In large or small ways, we all come to moments of deep distress: a doctor's report, a broken engagement, a poor personal choice, a shift in the stock market, a relational betrayal, a corporate down-size, or one of a million other unexpected events. In these times, the blue skies of life can seem to disappear behind the clouds of our circumstances and a chilly uncertainty runs down our spine. We begin to wonder if there is a way through the pain and heartache of what's ahead. We look down at the fuel gauge on the console of our life and it registers "empty." We might feel emotionally depleted, physically exhausted, relationally hopeless, spiritually barren, or mentally fatigued.

In these times the enemy of our soul wants to whisper, with sinister intent, "You will never make it. This is the end of the road for you."

God speaks a radically different message. Through his Word, by his Holy Spirit, and through the lives of wonderful examples, God declares with heavenly wisdom, "You'll get through this. It won't be painless. It won't be quick. But I will use this mess for good. In the meantime, don't be foolish or naive. But don't despair either."

How are you doing today? Have you hit the wall? Have you

bonked? Does your challenge appear insurmountable? If so, there is a story you absolutely have to hear. It is about a young man named Joseph who discovered that God is near even when it seems there is no way to make it through.

In the six sessions of this small group journey, you will learn that God is ready and able to help you, whatever your dilemma. If you don't believe it, just ask Joseph—you will find him at the bottom of a pit.

You'll Get Through This

Introduction

No one travels far down the road of life without discovering that this journey is not always smooth or perfect. We can pray and wish for safety on the way. We should enjoy the stretches of the ride when the sun shines and things go beautifully. We ought to thank God for the times when we find ourselves singing, whistling, laughing, and smiling as we travel along.

But every single human being has discovered that there are bumps, detours, and even collisions that can bring our joy to a screeching halt. This is not fatalism. It is not negativity. It is certainly not a lack of faith. It is life on this planet.

If you meet someone—a preacher, teacher, or sales person—who tries to tell you otherwise, BEWARE! If someone is peddling promises of a life with endlessly calm seas, perpetual blue skies, freedom from back pain, a guarantee of financial security, and ear-to-ear smiles all of your days, be very, very careful.

The Bible is filled with faithful friends of God who suffered in this life. Moses was violently opposed by the people he spent his life loving and trying to lead. David learned to dodge spears hurled at him by a mad king. Ruth walked through the death of her husband and became a stranger in a strange land. Jeremiah was beaten and thrown into a pit. Stephen, an early church leader, was stoned to death. The apostle Paul was strapped up and beaten no less than five times. The list could go on and on.

Then there is Joseph. He discovered at a young age that the road of life is not always smooth. His story is peppered with rejection, false attacks, deceitful accusations, enslavement, imprisonment, and long stretches of loneliness.

If you have ever hit a hard patch of road and thought, "I'll never get through this," you just might want to look over Joseph's shoulder and learn from his journey. It was hard. It was not a weekend trip but a tour of duty that lasted about two decades! But his story echoes through the centuries to remind us that we can make it through even the toughest of times. We really can.

> You'll get through this. It won't be painless. It won't be quick. But God will use this mess for good. In the meantime, don't be foolish or naive. But don't despair either. With God's help, you will get through this.

Talk About It

Tell about a situation you faced during which you felt, "I don't think I will ever make it through this." How did you feel when you made it through?

Video Teaching Notes

As you watch the video teaching segment for session 1 featuring Max Lucado, use the following outline to record anything that stands out to you.

Ordinary people face very real pain!

Meeting Joseph's family, with all their warts

Spending time in a cistern

You meant it for evil, God re-wove it

The truth of the matter:

It won't be painless

It won't be quick

God will use this mess for good

Video Discussion and Bible Study

1. In the video, Max talks about the hard times we face on life's journey, and he says, "God will use this mess for good." How have you experienced this in your life?

Read: Genesis 37:12–24

2. Tell about a time you ended up in a cistern and how you got there. How did you feel while you were in the cistern? How did you plead with God and even with people in an effort to get out of that painful situation?

3. If you are in a cistern right now, briefly share the situation (if you feel comfortable doing so) and how your group members can support and care for you in this time.

Read: Genesis 37:1–11

4. Some of the pain we face in life comes from the very people who should love and care for us—our family. This was certainly true for Joseph. What dysfunctions and unhealthy patterns in Joseph's family led to heartache and pain?

5. When you consider the road of life you have traveled thus far, how has your family (or maybe your church family) caused you pain and heartache? (Please refrain from using specific names; simply share generally about the experience.) Why do these wounds pierce so deeply?

6. There are many ways we can respond when thrown into a pit by family, friends, strangers, or life's circumstances. What are some of the typical responses?

God will use your mess for good. We see a perfect mess; God sees a perfect chance to train, test, and teach.

Read: Genesis 50:19–21

7. Years after Joseph's brothers threw him into a cistern, their father dies and they fear that Joseph will at last exact revenge. What do you learn about Joseph's heart and outlook on life as you read his response in this critical moment? What can you learn from his example?

8. If you were in Joseph's shoes and came to a point where those who had hurt you were now under your power, how do you think you would have responded?

Now, replace the hypothetical scenario with a real situation in your life. How do you believe God wants you to respond to and treat someone who has hurt you?

9. Max talks about how God re-wove the evil planned by Joseph's brothers and redeemed it for heavenly good. How has God re-woven something that was done to you with evil intent? What good did he bring from it?

> What Satan intends for evil, God, the Master Weaver and Master Builder, redeems for good.

10. Joseph's journey from a cistern in his teenage years to finally becoming a man of influence in Pharaoh's court lasted about twenty years. How did walking a hard road over time shape Joseph's character and outlook on life?

How has God used a journey of struggle in your life to shape who you are today? How have you looked up and seen God and drawn closer to him through your times in a pit?

Closing Prayer

Spend time in your group praying in any of the following directions:

- Turn your voice and eyes upward in prayer and ask for the ability to see the face of Jesus looking at you as you do.
- Ask God to be with your group members in the cisterns of life and pray for an attitude of grace, even in the darkest pits.
- Lift up prayers of forgiveness for those who have thrown you into a cistern, whether recently or as far back as childhood.
- Invite the Holy Spirit to unleash his power to re-weave the evil intents of others and bring good from them.

God gets us through stuff. *Through* is a favorite word of God's: "When you pass through the waters, I will be with you; and through the rivers, they shall not overflow you. When you walk through the fire, you shall not be burned, nor shall the flame scorch you" (Isaiah 43:2 NKJV).

Between Sessions

Look Back Down the Road

Reflecting on your life, identify as many as three cisterns in which you have spent time. Then ponder the person who had a hand in putting you there. Pray for a heart of forgiveness toward these people. Also, think about how God has used their intended evil and turned it toward his glory and good.

Cistern #1

What cistern was I thrown into?

How can I pray for the person(s) who put me there and grow in grace toward them?

How was God with me in that dark time?

What good did God bring through this bad situation? How has God shaped and formed me through what I experienced?

Cistern #2

What cistern was I thrown into?

How can I pray for the person(s) who put me there and grow in grace toward them?

How was God with me in that dark time?

What good did God bring through this bad situation? How has God shaped and formed me through what I experienced?

Cistern #3

What cistern was I thrown into?

How can I pray for the person(s) who put me there and grow in grace toward them?

How was God with me in that dark time?

What good did God bring through this bad situation? How has God shaped and formed me through what I experienced?

Let Vengeance Belong to God

If you have been harboring judgment, anger, or bitterness toward someone who wronged you in the past, reconsider Joseph's story as well as Romans 12:17–21:

> Do not repay anyone evil for evil. Be careful to do what is right in the eyes of everyone. If it is possible, as far as it depends on you, live at peace with everyone. Do not take revenge, my dear friends, but leave room for God's wrath, for it is written: "It is mine to avenge; I will repay," says the Lord. On the contrary: "If your enemy is hungry, feed him; if he is thirsty, give him something to drink. In doing this, you will heap burning coals on his head." Do not be overcome by evil, but overcome evil with good.

> God cares about justice more than we do.

Self-Examination

Family history can repeat itself. Far too often the abused becomes the abuser, the neglected becomes the neglector, and sins are passed down to the next generation. Make a list of some of the patterns, sins, and dysfunctions that existed in your home as you grew up. Actually take time to write them down:

-
-
-
-
-

Next, look over this list and do three things:

1. Pray that you will not repeat these patterns in your family.
2. Get help from a pastor or Christian counselor if you have already begun to repeat the sins of the past.
3. As the Lord leads, talk with parents, siblings, or other family members who have hurt you and seek to build bridges of restoration and healing.

| History is redeemed, not in minutes, but in lifetimes.

Journal

Use the space provided below to write reflections on any of the following topics:

- Ways you can extend grace and forgiveness, even to those who have thrown you into a cistern
- How God has shaped and formed you into the person you are today, even through the hard times (especially through the hard times)
- How God has been with you in the cisterns and pits of your life

Recommended Reading

As you consider what you have learned in this session, read chapter 1 of the book *You'll Get Through This* by Max Lucado. In preparation for session 2, you might want to read chapter 2.

Down and Out, but Never Alone

Introduction

In the first *Rocky* movie, the climax comes near the end of the film when an unknown Italian southpaw gets a chance to box the reigning heavyweight champion. Apollo Creed, the flamboyant titleholder, sees the fight as an exhibition more than a serious boxing match. He plans to dance around the ring, give his opponent a chance to have his moment in the spotlight, entertain the crowds, and then knock out Rocky. The problem is, no one told Rocky Balboa, the "Italian Stallion," that it was a show. He came to fight.

In the first round, Rocky catches Apollo Creed with the full force of a left uppercut and Apollo hits the mat like a sack of wheat. It is the first time he has ever been knocked down in a fight. When he gets to his feet he begins to beat on Rocky mercilessly, but the challenger simply won't stay down. He won't quit.

When the bell sounds for the second round, these two men go to war. They exchange punches over the next twelve rounds and Rocky is on the receiving end of most of them.

By the fourteenth round, Rocky is stumbling around the ring like a drunken man. Then Creed floors him with a fierce right upper-cut that sends him sprawling to the mat. The referee begins the ten-count as Rocky tries to stand. His face is swollen and bloody, his body is beaten, and his energy reserves have been on empty for at least three rounds. His trainer, Mickey, screams, "Down! Down! Stay down!" He pleads with Rocky to just give in to the inevitable and stay on the mat.

But as the referee gets to "nine," Rocky staggers to his feet. The crowd chants his name over and over again. Apollo, who has thrown his hands in the air as a declaration of victory, looks over at Rocky in disbelief. The fight continues. Rocky pounds the champ with a shattering punch that cracks his ribs just as the bell sounds to end the fourteenth round.

In Rocky's corner, the fatigued and relentless boxer's eye is so puffy that he can't see. He orders Mickey, "Cut me." In Apollo's corner, his trainer tells the champ, "You're bleeding inside; I'm gonna stop the fight." The injured champ responds with fierce determination, "You ain't stopping nothing! You ain't stopping nothing!" Just before the bell sounds to bring the two boxers back to the center of the ring, Rocky says to his trainer, "You stop this fight, I'll kill you." By the end of the fifteenth and final round, both fighters are standing—but barely!

This movie won three Oscars, including best picture of 1976. It was made on a budget of 1.1 million dollars and was filmed in twenty-eight days. But it eventually made over 225 million dollars and inspired six more *Rocky* films.

There is something compelling about a person with an unquenchable spirit. We are drawn to those who won't give up, won't give in, and won't stay down on the mat. In our hearts, all of us wish we had the strength and courage to get back up on our feet when life has knocked us down ... again.

| You'll get through this, what a bold statement! |

Talk About It

Give an example of a movie or book character with an unquench-able spirit and shocking resiliency when faced with powerful adver-sity. Why are people drawn to a character like this?

Video Teaching Notes

As you watch the video teaching segment for session 2 featuring Max Lucado, use the following outline to record anything that stands out to you.

Bounce back like Bozo

Joseph, an ancient, biblical Bozo

Joseph's dreams

From the heights to the depths in a matter of hours—have you ever been there?

Going down, down, down

Your destiny—what keeps you on your feet when life tries to knock you down?

What do you have that you can't lose?

Believe in God's destiny for you.

Video Discussion and Bible Study

1. Tell about a person you know who has a Bozo-like resiliency and seems able to bounce back and stay on their feet even when life tries to knock them down. What is it in a person that fortifies them and empowers them to keep getting up when many people would throw in the towel and stay on the mat?

2. Describe a time you were dealt a powerful blow that could have knocked you out, but your faith in God gave you strength to get back up again. How did your faith carry you through?

Read: Genesis 37:5–11

3. What do you think Joseph's dreams taught him about himself and his future?

4. How did Joseph's family members respond to his dreams?

How do you think you would have responded had you been one of Joseph's older brothers and he told you these dreams?

5. Joseph knew that God had a destiny for his life. He was confident that one day he would have a place of influence and impact—God had shown him this. How does knowing that God has a plan for our lives help us bounce back when times get dark, painful, and just plain hard?

What has God shown you about his plan and destiny for your life that could help you stand strong in difficult times?

Read: Genesis 37:23–28

6. If you were Joseph, what might have been going through your mind as your brothers plotted and then sold you as a slave? What might you have felt as you were walking in a caravan, looking back as your brothers, homeland, and dreams disappeared over the horizon?

> Don't get sucked into short-term thinking. Your struggles will not last forever, but you will.

7. Joseph begins Genesis 37 as the favored son, the recipient of dreams predicting his prominence, and a special assignment from his father. By the end of the chapter he has been stripped of his beautiful robe, rejected by his brothers, and sold as a slave. Tell about a time your own life took a radical shift in a short period of time. How was your faith impacted by this sudden and unexpected change of events?

Read: Ephesians 1:3; John 15:13–16; 1 Peter 1:18–20; and
2 Corinthians 5:1

8. When the apostle Paul tells the believers in Ephesus that God has "blessed [them] with every spiritual blessing in the heavenly places in Christ" (NKJV), what does he mean? Make a list of some spiritual blessings we have through faith in Jesus.

-
-
-
-
-
-
-
-

How could a deep and abiding awareness of these blessings help a Christian stand strong in hard times?

9. Jesus tells his followers that they are his loved and chosen children. How can a firm conviction that we are precious and valued children of God help us through the tough seasons of life?

God chose you. The choice wasn't obligatory, required, compulsory, forced, or compelled. He selected you because he wanted to.

10. How can a firm conviction that heaven is our home and we will spend eternity with our loving heavenly Father help us bounce back and stay on our feet in the challenging times of life?

Closing Prayer

Spend time in your group praying in any of the following directions:

- Thank God that heaven is your eternal home and destination through faith in Jesus, and pray that this reality will fortify and strengthen you in the hard times of life.
- Thank God that he has a plan and destiny for your life. Pray that it will become clearer with each passing day.
- Lift up friends and family members who are in a time of going down, down, down. If they are Christians, pray that they will remember who they are—chosen and loved children of God.
- Celebrate the reality and hope of heaven. Praise God for opening the way to eternity with him through the death and resurrection of Jesus.

Between Sessions

Honor a Bozo in Your Life!

God has placed one or more people in each of our lives who are resilient, long-suffering, and who have bounced back from more tough times than Bozo himself. These people inspire us and give us hope.

In the coming week, write a note to one such person in your life and thank them for demonstrating tenacious faith in hard times. Let them know that you see God alive in their heart and life.

Helping a Friend Who Is Feeling Down, Down, Down

If a member of your small group is experiencing a time when they are feeling down and things seem to be getting worse, contact them this coming week. Ask them three questions:

1. How can I pray for you during this time?
2. How can I serve you in the coming days? (Be sure to follow through.)
3. Do you realize that you are a loved and cherished child of God? (If they have forgotten, take time to remind them.)

Dare to Write It Down

God gave Joseph a vision of what would be. It took decades for the dream to become a reality. But it did!

Likewise, God has given you moments when you have had a picture of how he wants to work in and through your life. Briefly list these moments on a sheet of paper and put it in your Bible. Or type it into a document on your phone and keep it with you wherever you go. When you wonder if you can make it through a challenging time, read this list and remember God's plan for your life.

> You are God's child. He saw you, picked you, and placed you. "You did not choose me. I chose you" (John 15:16 NLT).

Journal

Use the space provided below to write reflections on any of the following topics:

- Write the names of a few people in your life who have exhibited resilient faith. Make a list of ways you have seen them hold the hand of Jesus as they have walked through hard times.
- List some of the dreams God has given you and how you believe he wants to work in and through your life for his glory.

- Continue adding to your list from question 8 more things that you have, through faith in Jesus, which no one can ever take away.

Recommended Reading

As you reflect on the lessons of this session, read chapter 2 of the book *You'll Get Through This* by Max Lucado. In preparation for session 3, you might want to read chapters 3–4.

Stupid Won't Fix Stupid

Introduction

Have you ever watched people play dominos? There are really two ways to play. Older people know the rules, sit at tables, lay the pieces flat so they can match the dots to corresponding dots, and keep score. Kids, in general, play a very different game. They don't know or care about the rules. They lie on the ground and carefully set up the dominos on their edges, standing tall like soldiers in a row. Some kids might even get fancy and make the row of dominos twist and turn around their bedroom floor.

Once the dominos are all standing, the big moment comes. With excitement and anticipation they push one domino and watch as, click, click, click, the dominos all tumble over. No rules, no score, just a chain reaction of dominos scattered all over the bedroom.

Sometimes, in times of struggle and pain, Satan invites us to play his own sinister version of dominos. Peter warns us that the enemy of our souls prowls around like a roaring lion seeking someone to devour (1 Peter 5:8). When we are tired, weary, and disheartened, the devil is always lurking in the shadows. He wants to entice us to make one small choice that will have long-term repercussions. Just one pill, one lie, one financial corner cut, one drink, one night of "pleasure," or one unwise decision and ... click, click, click, the dominos fall. In these moments, a single choice can start a chain reaction that will cost more than we could ever dream.

One bite of forbidden fruit impacted the entire human race. One moment of weakness could change the direction of your life. Satan knows this. He also understands that we are more susceptible to temptation when we are tired, worn, discouraged, disheartened, and feeling like, "I'll never get through this."

In times like this we must be on our guard. Temptation is near. Sin can look a little more enticing. Satan is on the prowl.

Don't push that first domino. Life is not a game.

Do what pleases God. Nothing more, nothing less.

Talk About It

How have you seen the enemy seek to entice and tempt you in times when you were tired, worn, or feeling discouraged? Why do you think Satan attacks so frequently in these times of life?

Video Teaching Notes

As you watch the video teaching segment for session 3 featuring Max Lucado, use the following outline to record anything that stands out to you.

When dumb becomes dumber

Joseph becomes influential and powerful

Temptation comes crashing in—for Joseph and us!

It is easy to excuse sin in the hard times of life: rationalization

Look honestly at the chain reaction and consequences of saying yes to temptation

Do what pleases God

The blessings of hanging in there and saying no to temptation

You will never go where God is not.

Video Discussion and Bible Study

1. Max is honest and vulnerable in this video section, telling a story about a time he did something he considered "stupid." He did not listen to advice or heed the warning signs around him. He kept going full throttle and ran aground on his own folly and stubbornness. Tell an honest story about a time when you raced past warning signs and ended up in a mess. How did you feel when this happened? What were some of the consequences and repercussions of your actions?

Read: Genesis 39:1–6

2. Joseph was betrayed by his brothers, thrown into a pit, sold as a slave, exiled far from his loved ones and homeland, and then sold again. He was a stranger in a strange land. Yet, through all of this, he was not alone. How do you see God present and at work in Joseph's life, even in this very painful time?

How have you experienced God being with you when your life journey has been hard and painful?

3. When times are tough, what are some the tactics the enemy uses to entice us to make a bad choice and push that first domino?

How have you personally seen temptations increase in times when you feel exhausted, worn, beat down, and generally discouraged?

| Don't make matters worse by doing something you'll regret. |

4. What are some specific ways we can fortify our souls, setting up hedges against the enemy's enticements when we feel discouraged and particularly susceptible to attack?

How can your small group become a source of support when you are facing spiritual attacks?

| You represent a challenge to Satan's plan. |

Read: Genesis 39:6–12

5. Some temptations lie outside of our normal reach. We have to really go after them and find our way into trouble. Other temptations don't bother knocking—they just invite themselves in and interrupt our lives. What kind of enticement did Joseph face and how did he seek to navigate around it? What did Joseph learn about temptations in this season of his life?

What are some of the best tactics you have discovered to help a Christian fight against bold, pushy, persistent, in-your-face kinds of temptation?

6. When we feel abandoned, discouraged, sick, or tired, rationalization can also come creeping into our minds and hearts. Respond to this statement: *The human heart has the ability to rationalize almost anything given the right (or wrong) circumstances!*

Justifications and rationalizations can pop up like weeds after a summer rain.

7. Joseph refused to accept the enticement of Potiphar's wife because he wanted to honor his master Potiphar, who had elevated him in the household and had entrusted him with significant responsibility. How can thinking about the people who will be impacted by our sin help us resist temptation?

How can writing down and thinking about all the repercussions and consequences of sin help us resist moments of temptation?

| Joseph placed his loyalty above lusts. |

Read: Psalm 51:1–4 and Genesis 39:9

8. Both King David (the writer of Psalm 51) and Joseph had a deep sense that any sin they committed would ultimately be against God. How is all sin truly an offense against God? Why is it important that we consider the heart of God when we are tempted to make a sinful decision?

Read: Genesis 39:13–21

9. Joseph did everything right. He resisted; he refused to rationalize; and when the heat was on, he ran. What were the final results of Joseph's commitment to holiness and honoring God?

Tell about a time you tried to do everything right but things seemed to turn out all wrong.

You will never go wrong doing what is right.

10. Max makes this statement: "Egypt can be a cruddy place. It can be a petri dish for brainless decisions." What is an Egypt you are facing right now? What are some of the potentially "brainless decisions" you need to be careful to avoid at this time of your life? How can your group members pray for you as you walk through this time?

Closing Prayer

Spend time in your group praying in any of the following directions:

- Pray for wisdom to notice when you are starting to rationalize sin rather than repent of it.
- Ask the Holy Spirit to give you eyes to see when the enemy is attacking your life, be it overt or covert.
- Lift up a group member who is facing a challenging time. Ask God to fortify them, protect them, and give them strength to avoid making things worse by falling for any form of temptation the enemy might send their way.
- Pray for all of your group members to become people who are passionate about doing what pleases God.

Between Sessions

Building a Strong Fortification

In ancient times, cities would build huge walls or dig moats as a line of defense against enemies. As followers of Jesus, we need to fortify our lives against the enticements, temptations, or flat-out attacks of the enemy of our soul. One of the best ways to do this is to seek strength in numbers. We do not have to stand or fight alone.

Consider some of these ideas that might help fortify the defenses around your heart and life:

- Join a men's or women's group (or find an accountability partner) and create a place where you can be honest about the struggles you face as you seek to walk with Jesus in the easy and hard times of life.
- Invite godly friends and family members to pray for you when you are facing a difficult time.
- Memorize two or three passages of Scripture to strengthen yourself when facing a specific area of temptation: for example, sexual lust, greed, or selfishness. Use a Bible concordance or do an Internet search to find applicable references.

Lay claim to the nearness of God. "Never will I leave you; never will I forsake you" (Hebrews 13:5).

Make a List

Max talks about the value of making a list of all the people who would be hurt and impacted by your sin. It is also helpful to look at other potential collateral damage such as the impact on your reputation, finances, etc. Try this exercise with two or three areas of sin you regularly confront.

If I were to follow the enemy's enticement to _____
and this became public and known by all …

Consequences for family members:

Consequences for friends:

Consequences for other people in my life:

Consequences for my reputation:

Consequences for my finances:

Consequences for my future:

If I were to follow the enemy's enticement to _____
and this became public and known by all ...

Consequences for family members:

Consequences for friends:

Consequences for other people in my life:

Consequences for my reputation:

Consequences for my finances:

Consequences for my future:

If I were to follow the enemy's enticement to _____ and this became public and known by all ...

Consequences for family members:

Consequences for friends:

Consequences for other people in my life:

Consequences for my reputation:

Consequences for my finances:

Consequences for my future:

Sing It Out

There is something powerful in a song. When the lyrics are locked in your mind and heart, something beautiful can happen. Max tells the story of Thomas Dorsey and the turning point that occurred in his life when God put a song on his heart. People have drawn strength and comfort from that song for almost seventy years!

Find a few great hymns or powerful praise choruses and commit their tune and words to memory. When times are hard and temptation is near, try singing. Seriously, try it. God might just infuse that moment with the power of his Holy Spirit and set you free from temptation as he sweeps you into his presence in worship.

Journal

Use the space provided below to write reflections on any of the following topics:

- Note some of the repetitive ways the enemy seeks to entice and tempt you. Look for a pattern.
- List some of your most common rationalizations when facing temptations in hard times.
- Ask this question: "If I were the devil, where would I attack me?" Then write down three or four ways you can fortify this specific area of your life.

Recommended Reading

As you reflect on what you have learned in this session, read chapter 4 of the book *You'll Get Through This* by Max Lucado. In preparation for session 4, you might want to read chapters 5–8.

Is God Good When Life Isn't?

Introduction

It is a simple Latin phrase, only three words: *quid pro quo.*

Roughly translated, it means, "This for that." This little phrase encapsulates the way many people approach life. Everything is a negotiation, a contract, an agreement. You do this; I'll do that—everyone is happy!

Marriages can function like this. You clean the house and raise the kids and I'll go to the office and pay the bills. You listen to me and show tenderness and I'll respond with romantic affection. You scratch my back and I'll scratch yours. *Quid pro quo.*

Business partnerships often rest on this line of thinking. You handle the clients and I'll do the bookkeeping. You put in sixty hours a week and I'll match it. You keep the customers happy and I'll keep product on the shelves. This for that. *Quid pro quo.*

Friendships can even revolve around this philosophy. If you are there for me in my times of need, I will be there for you. When you show kindness and concern, so will I. If you speak well of me to others, my words will be equally flattering about you. *Quid pro quo.*

For some people, *quid pro quo* makes their world go round.

But here is the dilemma with this contractual approach to relationships: when a spouse does not uphold his or her part of the bargain, then all bets are off. When a business partner is not producing the goods, it might be time to offload them. When a friend is not measuring up and caring as we think they should, we can find ourselves moving on to greener relational pastures.

Nowhere is this kind of thinking more dangerous than when we try to import it into our relationship with God. When we impose on God our sense of how he should behave, what he should do for us, or how he should run the universe, things can get messy very quickly.

God, if you keep my body healthy, then I will follow you with all my heart. If you give me a solid financial footing and provide what I think I need, then I will lovingly share my resources with others. If you protect my children from harm, then I will follow you and trust you. If you draw my loved ones to faith in you, then I will tell the world that you are a good and merciful God. *Quid pro quo.*

But when your health fails, your finances crash, your child is seriously injured, or a loved one dies without faith in Jesus, what then? Is God still good? Will you still follow him with all your heart?

Talk About It

How can using a *quid pro quo* approach to relationships be helpful? When does it become detrimental and harmful? How can a *quid pro quo* approach to faith cause real problems in our relationship with God?

Video Teaching Notes

As you watch the video teaching segment for session 4 featuring Max Lucado, use the following outline to record anything that stands out to you.

When tragedy strikes, and strikes, and strikes!

Is God still good when ... ?

A contractual relationship with God?

Joseph meets Pharaoh

The sovereignty of God

God is not the author of evil

God does rule the universe

God permits

God can bring good out of all things

Can I love and trust God no matter what? No deal and no contracts!

God is not *sometimes* sovereign. He is not *occasionally* victorious. He does not occupy the throne one day and vacate it the next.

Video Discussion and Bible Study

1. Tell about a season when it felt like bad news, hard times, and painful circumstances just kept pounding your life like waves on the shore. How was your faith tested, and what helped you to remain faithful during this season?

2. Max tells the tragic and painful story of his friends Brian and Christyn Taylor. In her blog, Christyn wrote about a one-sided deal she had with God. She would endure trials as long as God did not push her past her stopping point. She wrote, "God knew where my line had been drawn and I knew in my heart he would never cross it." What are common "stopping points" that some Christians live with?

   What is the danger of saying, "I will love God and follow him as long as he never allows _____"? (You fill in the blank.)

3. Describe something that happened to you (or someone you care about) that you were sure God would never allow. How did you navigate the pain and uncertainty of that time?

> This season in which you find yourself may puzzle you, but it does not bewilder God. He can use it for his purpose.

Read: Malachi 3:6 and Hebrews 13:8

4. Why is it so easy to say, "God is good," when things are going our way but harder to declare that "God is good" when pain and tragedy crash into our lives?

If God is the same in both good and hard times, why do we see him in such different lights?

Read: Genesis 41:1–16, 25–36

5. In the video, Max says that "Joseph lived with an unshakable and deep-seated belief in God's sovereignty." How do you see this demonstrated in how Josvph spoke to and interacted with Pharaoh?

Do you believe, deep in your soul, that God is on the throne and really does rule the whole universe? If so, why do you have this confidence? If not, why do you doubt it?

Read: Job 34:10; James 1:16–17; and 1 John 4:8

6. Christians believe that God is the author of good and not of evil. We believe God is love. What is the difference between believing that God causes evil and that he permits it?

God, at times, permits tragedies. He allows Satan to unleash calamity. But he doesn't allow Satan to triumph.

Read: Romans 8:28

8. Max contends that God can take something evil, mix it with other ingredients, and bring something beautiful out of it. Do you agree with this? Why or why not?

How have you experienced God bringing good out of something that was clearly evil and not caused by God?

This is the repeated pattern in Scripture. *Evil. God. Good.*

Read: Romans 8:18–21

9. How does the hope of heaven and the assurance of God's ultimate victory help us in times when we don't understand the pain and sorrow we face in this life?

Your pain won't last forever, but you will. "Whatever we may have to go through now is less than nothing compared with the magnificent future God has planned for us" (Romans 8:18 PH).

10. How does God want to fortify and strengthen us through Christian community during our tough times? What can you do to make your small group become a place where supportive community is normative?

Closing Prayer

Spend time in your group praying in any of the following directions:

- Confess where your faith has become a *quid pro quo* contractual agreement, and ask for faith to love and follow God no matter what.
- Thank God for the times you have seen him bring good out of experiences that seemed would yield only pain.
- Ask for patience for yourself and other group members as you continue to walk through times of loss and sorrow.
- Praise God that he is sovereign and on the throne, even when you can't see it or understand what is happening in your life or the world.

God promises to render beauty out of "all things," not "each thing." (The isolated events may be evil, but the ultimate culmination is good.)

Between Sessions

Bring Grace and Care

In the book of Job we read that when this great man of faith endured unthinkable loss and sorrow, three of his friends came to be with him. These friends behaved miserably later in the story, but when they first arrived, they actually did a good job of caring.

> When Job's three friends, Eliphaz the Temanite, Bildad the Shuhite and Zophar the Naamathite, heard about all the troubles that had come upon him, they set out from their homes and met together by agreement to go and sympathize with him and comfort him. When they saw him from a distance, they could hardly recognize him; they began to weep aloud, and they tore their robes and sprinkled dust on their heads. Then they sat on the ground with him for seven days and seven nights. No one said a word to him, because they saw how great his suffering was (Job 2:11–13).

We all know people who, like Job, are walking through a time of heart-wrenching loss and pain. Identify someone you know who is in such a season and reach out to them. Don't give theological answers; don't try to make everything better; simply find time to be with them. Sometimes just "being there" is the best care that we can offer.

Watch Your Language

When Joseph stood before Pharaoh and interpreted his dreams, he used a lot of "God language." When asked to interpret the dreams, Joseph was quick to say, "I cannot do it." But on the heels of this statement Joseph declared, "But God will give Pharaoh the answer he desires" (Genesis 41:16). Three more times Joseph directed the discussion to God. He was not going to let this be about him. He would not take credit for what God was about to do.

During the coming week, make an effort to listen to what you say. Are you more me-centered or more God-centered? Do you direct conversations to focus on who you are, what you did, and all that you have accomplished? Or are you quick to let people know that God is alive and working in your life and our world? Perhaps your self-study will cause you to shine the light in a different direction.

Count Your Blessings

There is a wonderful old hymn, "Count Your Blessings," written by Johnson Oatman Jr., to encourage Christians to remember all God has done for them. If you don't know this song, find it in a hymnal or on the Internet. Read the words. Reflect on the message. If you know the tune, sing the song!

Then, over the coming week, write down 25 – 50 blessings you have experienced in the last twelve months. Meditate on these. Thank God for them. Let others know how good God has been (even in the hard times). Then, start over and count even more blessings.

Gratitude always leaves us looking at God and away from dread. It does to anxiety what the morning sun does to valley mist: it burns it up.

Journal

Use the space provided below to write reflections on any of the following topics:

- Finish this statement, over and over again: "I know that God is good, even when ..."
- Write down some of the ways you have seen and experienced the sovereign hand of God at work in your life and the world around you.
- Write a prayer of thanksgiving and praise to God. Focus on his goodness, even when times are hard and answers are difficult to find.

Recommended Reading

As you consider what you have learned in this session, read chapters 7–8 of the book *You'll Get Through This* by Max Lucado. In preparation for session 5, you might want to read chapters 9–11.

Now, About Those Family Scandals and Scoundrels

Introduction

It was around Christmas 2010 when the trend really took off. Christmas card companies must have noticed. Rather than traditional cards with a short family update and a personal signature, something different showed up in many mailboxes. Over the next couple of years the trend increased.

Family photos and portraits became the rage. A beautiful, almost magic moment captured in digital format, printed out, and sent to friends and family far and wide. A picture taken in the woods, at the beach, in the living room, or at a studio became very popular. With one "click," a perfect family for all to see.

Here is the truth about that family photo: that's as good as it gets!

If you could have been there for the half-hour before or the day after the photo shoot, the picture might have been slightly different—not quite as perfect! Here is the reality behind many of these moments captured and sent to friends or blown up and hung on a living room wall: they do not tell the whole story.

The whole family had to wait for the baby to stop crying, then to be changed, then to be fed—just to get that calm moment to snap off the picture.

Two teenagers were bribed with a lunch at their favorite restaurant just to get them there. They really did not want to miss time with their friends on a Saturday.

The husband with his arm wrapped tenderly around his wife's shoulder has not willingly embraced her during the previous week because things said in a fight they had still run through his mind.

None of the kids really wanted to wear the clothes Mom had picked out, and she was frustrated because each child told her so.

It took over an hour and more than twenty tries to get everyone to smile (or appear to be smiling).

A fight between siblings erupted during the picture-taking ordeal. No one could figure out what was really going on, but one of them kept yelling, "She keeps touching me!"

But then, at just the right moment, in the eye of the storm, "Click!"

Got it! Print it! Mail it (or email it) for everyone to see. The perfect family.

In reality, no family is as all-together and glossy as it appears in these family photos. Every family has its moments, bumps, fights, struggles, and skeletons. We just don't take pictures at those moments and mail them to everyone we know.

Talk About It

If you have gone through the family photo experience, what interesting memories come to mind?

Video Teaching Notes

As you watch the video teaching segment for session 5 featuring Max Lucado, use the following outline to record anything that stands out to you.

No perfect families, not even in the Bible!

The danger of ignoring past hurts

Restoration: God cares about it and so should we

Family reunion—not a pretty picture

Retribution and revenge: Should I or shouldn't I?

Honest evaluation

The road to healing

Restoration matters to God. The healing of the heart involves
the healing of the past.

Video Discussion and Bible Study

1. None of us comes from a perfect family. Describe some of
   the family challenges you encountered as a child and teenager
   growing up.

2. Max takes note of the fact that Joseph had the resources and
   ability to reconnect with his family back in Canaan and seek
   some kind of reconciliation. But he made no effort to do so. Max

says, "Joseph kept his family secrets a secret, untouched and untreated. Joseph was content to keep his past in the past." What are some potential dangers if we bury the painful and broken parts of our past and try to move on as if it they do not exist?

Read: Genesis 42:1–17

3. What do you see in Joseph's response to his brothers that shows he had not dealt with or resolved his pain from the past?

4. The last time Joseph saw his brothers, they had thrown him into a pit and were selling him as a slave. He had begged for mercy and received none. He was powerless and they had him outnumbered. What could have been going through his mind and heart during this current encounter?

If you had been in Joseph's shoes, how might you have responded when faced with your brothers asking you to provide for them in their time of need?

5. Respond to this statement: "Restoration is always a big deal to God. He will create situations and opportunities for us to choose healing over brokenness and restoration over retribution."

Tell about a situation in your life right now in which you are facing a choice between working at healing or leaving a relationship broken.

Sometimes God gives more than we request by going deeper than we ask.

Read: Genesis 42:18 – 32

6. In verse 24, we read that Joseph turned away from his brothers and wept. What do you think caused Joseph to respond with such deep emotion? When it comes to our own family history and struggles, why is it important for us to deal with our emotions and refuse to bury them?

7. Now the shoe is on the other foot. Joseph has power and authority, and his brothers are under his control. Despite this twist, how do you see Joseph's hurt still coming through? How do you see Joseph extend grace to his brothers?

Why is it so hard to extend grace to those who have hurt, rejected, or abused us?

8. "Hurt people hurt people!" It's a simple yet profound statement. How have you seen this reality in your relationships?

9. It is possible to stop the generational cycle of alcoholism, abuse, neglect, greed, or a thousand other sins. It is possible, through the power of the living God, to say, "It stops with me! I will not pass this on to the next generation!" What is one pattern, behavior, or sin in your family history that you do not want to see passed on to the next generation? What steps can you take to stop this pattern from poisoning your children? How can your group members pray for you and support you as you seek to break the cycle in this generation?

| Your history doesn't have to be your future. |

Read: Romans 12:1–2 and 2 Corinthians 5:17–20

10. What practical steps can we take to move toward a healed and reconciled relationship with people who have hurt us?

What is one specific step of reconciliation you believe God wants you to take with a family member or friend who has hurt you? When will you take this step, and how can your group members keep you accountable to follow through?

God not only wants your whole heart, he wants your heart whole.

Closing Prayer

Spend time in your group praying in any of the following directions:

- Thank God for the good memories and positive moments of your childhood and youth.
- Ask God to help you move toward healing and reconciliation in broken family relationships.
- Pray that you will respond with grace and mercy when you feel like retaliating and exacting revenge.
- Pray for the courage to see your family as it is and seek to make it better in the future.

Between Sessions

Honest Prayers and Laments

Max talks about the shift from a general prayer—"Lord, help me forgive"—to a very specific kind of prayer—"God, my mother neglected me, embarrassed me, and at times was abusive to me. I need help forgiving because I can't do it on my own."

Identify at least two areas in which you feel you were hurt by someone in your family. Pray as honestly as you can about what you experienced, how it felt, and the hurt you had (and still have) because of this experience. Ask God to help you learn how to forgive in your heart and extend grace to this person.

Revealing Leads to Healing: Facing My Scoundrels

Use the space below to work through a couple of experiences with family members who have been hurtful and unkind to you in some way. Pray that this process of revealing what you have experienced—to yourself and before God—will lead to healing in your heart and life.

Another Family Scoundrel (Write the initials of someone in your family who has hurt you):

Scandal (What did they do that was hurtful?):

Life Impact (How has the sin of this person affected your life?):

Possible Consequences (What could happen if you don't extend grace and seek forgiveness and reconciliation?):

Next Steps (What can you do to make a move toward healing and forgiveness?):

Another Family Scoundrel (Write the initials of someone in your family who has hurt you):

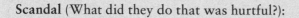

Scandal (What did they do that was hurtful?):

Life Impact (How has the sin of this person affected your life?):

Possible Consequences (What could happen if you don't extend grace and seek forgiveness and reconciliation?):

Next Steps (What can you do to make a move toward healing and forgiveness?):

Family Tree

Following a family tree and learning about one's ancestors has become very popular for some people. Here is a different kind of family tree exercise: Follow a sin or unhealthy pattern back through your family line. It could be substance abuse, racism, sexual sin, unfaithfulness, abuse, abandonment, radical materialism, or any other negative behavior you identify as prevalent.

Pick two different family patterns; then go backward and list any family members who have battled this tendency. Finally, consider a positive action you could take to reverse the trend.

Tree #1

Sin, pattern, or hurtful behavior:

Family member (and how this sin was lived out)

Family member (and how this sin was lived out)

Family member (and how this sin was lived out)

Family member (and how this sin was lived out)

Family member (and how this sin was lived out)

Personal Action Item: What is one action I can take to stop this pattern before it impacts the next generation?

Tree #2

Sin, pattern, or hurtful behavior:

Family member (and how this sin was lived out)

Family member (and how this sin was lived out)

Family member (and how this sin was lived out)

Family member (and how this sin was lived out)

Family member (and how this sin was lived out)

Personal Action Item: What is one action I can take to stop this pattern before it impacts the next generation?

> You don't have to give your kids what your ancestors gave you.

Journal

Use the space provided below to write reflections on any of the following topics:

- Write down at least five ways you have been positively shaped and influenced by being part of your family of origin.
- Write down a few ways your family has hurt you, but include some thoughts about how God has worked through the difficulty of those times to shape you more into the person he wants you to be.

- Record a prayer asking for God's healing touch and power in the broken and hurting parts of your heart.
- Make a list of steps you can take that will lead to restored relationships and reconciliation with people who have treated you in a hurtful way as you were growing up.

Note: The hurt and pain that comes from family can be very deep. As you walk through this session, if you feel there are still some deep and hidden issues to address, you might want to meet with your pastor or a Christian counselor to help you take additional steps forward.

Recommended Reading

As you reflect on what you have learned in this session, read chapters 9–11 of the book *You'll Get Through This* by Max Lucado. In preparation for session 6, you might want to read chapters 12–15.

God Can Use This for Good

Introduction

It is a winning formula used in more movies, TV shows, and books than you could track. The bad guy commits a crime—and we all know he is guilty. The good guy goes after him, chases him down, and corners him (this can take up most of a movie or chapters of a book). Then, in a flurry of bullets, an epic sword fight, an intricate court battle, or some other face-to-face confrontation, the bad guy goes down and there is vindication at last! The judgment is swift and the audience or reader drinks in the satisfaction of seeing the bad guy get what he deserves.

If the Bible followed this formula, then Joseph's response to his brothers would be very severe. They had abused him, abandoned him, sold him like a side of beef, and turned their backs on him when he cried out for mercy. But now Joseph is the prince of Egypt, in a place of power, and his brothers are weak and bowed down before him. Imagine the ending to this script, using the popular "good guy versus bad guy" motif:

BROTHERS (*Bowing down, whimpering, and begging for mercy*): We are starving and our family back in Canaan is in need. Please help us!

JOSEPH, PRINCE OF EGYPT (*Standing in regal authority looking down on his unsuspecting brothers*): I don't believe you. You are spies. Guards, surround them!

REUBEN, OLDEST BROTHER (*Still on the ground, but speaking for the family*): Your highness, trust me; we are brothers, sons of the same father. Our youngest brother is still at home, and one dear brother died many years ago. Please believe me. Trust us.

JOSEPH (*Eyes blazing with the fire of vengeance*): One of your brothers is dead? Really? Dead or betrayed? Tell me how your brother died!

SONS OF JACOB (*Camera pans their guilty faces, pressed against the marble floors of Pharaoh's palace*)

JOSEPH (*Shouting with angry judgment*): Your brother is dead? Are you sure? You are about to wish he were! I am Joseph. I am the one you abused, rejected, and sold as a slave. The last thing I did over two decades ago, as you sold me for twenty shekels of silver, was beg for mercy. Don't one of you dare ask for mercy now—there will be none. (*Nods at the soldiers*)

SOLDIERS OF PHARAOH'S PALACE (*Surrounding Joseph's brothers, they slowly lift their swords*)

Screen goes black

Seems like the ending to so many books and movies, doesn't it? But Joseph's ending is different, and so is ours—if we know Jesus.

The biblical story turns things upside down and surprises us. In God's story, vengeance is replaced with grace. Death is overcome by life. Judgment is swept aside so that forgiveness can win the day. If we listen to the biblical story, we find that the ending can be radically different.

> Forgive your enemies? That's where you and I come in. We forgive.

Talk About It

Tell about a favorite movie that follows the story line of the bad guys "getting what they deserve." Why is this a popular theme?

Video Teaching Notes

As you watch the video teaching segment for session 6 featuring Max Lucado, use the following outline to record anything that stands out to you.

The power of a great big brother

Joseph pours out his heart

Grace instead of judgment

Jesus our brother

Joseph and Jesus: Similarities and differences

God turns evil into good

Will you be a Joseph?

In God's hands, intended evil becomes eventual good.

Video Discussion and Bible Study

1. Tell a personal story about a big brother or big sister (or someone who functioned as such in your life) who cared for you and was there for you during a tough time.

Why is it so important and valuable to have people like this in your life?

Read: Genesis 45:1–15

2. What do you learn about Joseph's view of God from the way he responded to his brothers?

God, the Master Weaver. He stretches the yarn and intertwines the colors, the ragged twine with the velvet strings, the pains with the pleasures. Nothing escapes his reach. Every king, despot, weather pattern, and molecule is at his command. He passes the shuttle back and forth across the generations and, as he does, a design emerges. Satan weaves, God reweaves.

3. What parallels do you see in how Joseph responded to his brothers and how Jesus responds to us (even though we have sinned against him and rejected him)?

Read: Matthew 12:46–50 and Hebrews 2:10–13

4. What do these passages teach us about how Jesus sees us and how we are related to him through faith?

5. In the video, Max talked about how the sons of Jacob came to Egypt as poor and powerless men begging for food. But everything changed when they learned that the prince was their brother. How did their lot and future shift once they realized that the prince was Joseph and that he was ready to extend forgiveness and grace?

How does our life change when we receive Jesus as Savior and learn that we are no longer enemies of God but beloved children, and that Jesus is now our brother?

Jesus is the only picture of God ever taken.

Read: Matthew 11:28–30; 1 John 2:1–2; and Philippians 4:19

6. What do these passages and others like them teach you about how Jesus sees you? How does it make you feel when you realize that Jesus views you this way?

Read: Genesis 50:15–21

7. How do Joseph's brothers reveal that they still don't understand the gift of grace they have received from Joseph?

What does Joseph say and do to demonstrate he is very serious about walking in grace and not exacting revenge?

8. How do we act when we forget the depth and reality of God's grace given to us in Jesus Christ? How can fear, worry, and human good works start to slip into our relationship with Jesus if we forget the reality of his grace?

What can we do to keep from falling into fear-driven and works-based faith?

9. Max makes the bold statement, "God sees a Joseph in you." Then he says, "Your family needs a Joseph, a courier of grace in a day of anger and revenge!" How do you respond to these two statements?

Tell your group about one situation in your life when you had a chance to respond with grace and love rather than judgment and anger—and you came out on the side of grace. How did God show up in this situation?

You are a version of Joseph in your generation.

10. What is one way you can begin to be a bearer of grace in your family, as Joseph was in his?

How can your group members pray for you and encourage you as you seek to bring grace and the presence of Jesus into your family?

Closing Prayer

Spend time in your group praying in any of the following directions:

- Ask God to help you be a presence of grace and forgiveness in your family.
- Thank God for specific people who have been a loving big brother or sister to you (literally or spiritually).
- Pray for strength to extend grace rather than judgment to those who have wronged you.
- Praise Jesus for his atoning death and celebrate the astounding truth that he does not hold your sins against you but nailed them to the cross.

With Jesus, bad became good like night becomes day: regularly, reliably, refreshingly. And redemptively.

In the Coming Days

Come to Jesus

Take time to memorize these three short but powerful verses of the Bible, Matthew 11:28–30:

> [28] "Come to me, all you who are weary and burdened, and I will give you rest. [29] Take my yoke upon you and learn from me, for I am gentle and humble in heart, and you will find rest for your souls. [30] For my yoke is easy and my burden is light."

Hear Jesus invite you, even when you are weary—especially when you are weary. Ask him to help you experience the rest your soul longs for.

"House" Cleaning

Think back over your life, be it short or long. Reflect on different seasons and identify times when you have been hurt and may have not released this hurt to God. Admit where you may be nursing your pain and hoping for a "movie ending" in which you finally get vindication and revenge.

My Childhood:

My Adolescent Years:

My Early Adulthood:

My Adult Years:

Invite the Holy Spirit to show you where you are still holding on to hurt. Ask Jesus to help you extend forgiveness to the person who has wronged you in the same way Jesus has extended it to you. Pray for your heart to change. Ask God for a Joseph heart toward this person and for a Jesus ending to the story!

I'm Serious, I Forgive You

Joseph's brothers were not sure they were really forgiven. Yes, Joseph had told them. Yes, he had provided for them. But they wondered if this grace had an expiration date—specifically, when their father passed away. At that point, Joseph had to remind them that he really did love and forgive them.

If you have someone in your life who has wronged you and you have forgiven them, make sure that they know it. Tell them. Remind them. Be sure you are acting in a way that reveals the grace of Jesus. If it feels like the relationship has become strained, circle back and say that you know God is on the throne and his grace is enough for both of you!

Journal

Use the space provided below to write reflections on any of the following topics:

- Make a list of people who have been your spiritual big brothers and sisters. Write short prayers of thanks to God for these people.
- Pen a prayer of thanks for Jesus' forgiveness and grace that he has lavished on you. Then note some ways you can extend that grace to others.

- Write about what is causing you to feel weary and burdened these days, and then consider the ways that coming near to Jesus can lift these burdens and bring you rest.

Recommended Reading

As you reflect on what you have learned in this session, read chapters 12–15 from the book *You'll Get Through This* by Max Lucado.

Small Group Leader Helps

To ensure a successful small group experience, read the following information before beginning.

Group Preparation

Whether your small group has been meeting together for years or is gathering for the first time, be sure to designate a consistent time and place to work through the six sessions. Once you establish the when and where of your times together, select a facilitator who will keep discussions on track and an eye on the clock. If you choose to rotate this responsibility, assign the six sessions to their respective facilitators upfront, so that group members can prepare their thoughts and questions prior to the session they are responsible for leading. Follow the same assignment procedure should your group want to serve any snacks/beverages.

A Note to Facilitators

As facilitator, you are responsible for honoring the agreed-upon timeframe of each meeting, for prompting helpful discussion among your group, and for keeping the dialogue equitable by drawing out quieter members and helping more talkative members to remember that others' insights are valued in your group.

You might find it helpful to preview each session's video teaching segment (they range from 22–25 minutes) and then scan the discussion questions and Bible passages that pertain to it, highlighting various questions that you want to be sure to cover during your group's meeting. Ask God in advance of your time together to guide your group's discussion, and then be sensitive to the direction he wishes to lead.

Urge participants to bring their study guide, pen, and a Bible to every gathering. Encourage them to consider buying a copy of the book *You'll Get Through This* by Max Lucado to supplement this study.

Session Format

Each session of the study guide includes the following group components:

- **"Introduction"** — an entrée to the session's topic, which may be read by a volunteer or summarized by the facilitator
- **"Talk About It"** — an icebreaker question that relates to the session topic and invites input from every group member
- **"Video Teaching Notes"** — an outline of the session's video teaching segment for group members to follow along and take notes if they wish
- **"Video Discussion and Bible Study"** — video-related and Bible exploration questions that reinforce the session content and elicit personal input from every group member
- **"Closing Prayer"** — several prayer cues to guide group members in closing prayer

Additionally, in each session you will find a **"Between Sessions"** section (**"In the Coming Days"** for session 6) that includes suggestions for personal response, a journaling opportunity, and recommended reading from the *You'll Get Through This* book.

Tools for Your Church or Small Group

GRACE DVD-Based Study
978-1-4016-7582-0 | $39.99

Join Max Lucado through seven DVD
sessions ideal for small-group settings.

GRACE Participant's Guide
978-1-4016-7584-4 | $9.99

Filled with Scripture study, discussion
questions, and practical ideas designed
to lead group members to a deeper
understanding and application of grace,
this guide is an integral part of the
GRACE small-group study.

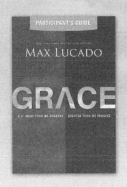

Shaped by Grace
978-0-8499-6450-3 | $2.99

Featuring key selections from *GRACE*,
this 64-page booklet is ideal for
introducing friends and family to the
transforming work of God's grace.

Inspired by what you just read?
Connect with Max.

Listen to Max's teaching ministry, UpWords, on the radio and online.
Visit www.MaxLucado.com to get FREE resources for spiritual
growth and encouragement, including:

- Archives of UpWords, Max's daily radio
  program, and a list of radio stations where it airs
- Devotionals and e-mails from Max
- First look at book excerpts
- Downloads of audio, video, and printed material
- Mobile content

You will also find an online store and special offers.

www.MaxLucado.com

1-800-822-9673

UpWords Ministries
P.O. Box 692170
San Antonio, TX 78269-2170

Join the Max Lucado community:

Follow Max on Twitter @MaxLucado
or at Facebook.com/UpWordsMinistry